the garden floor

the garden floor

DECORATIVE GROUNDWORK TO TRANSFORM YOUR GARDEN

JENNY HENDY

LORENZ BOOKS

This edition is published by Lorenz Books

Lorenz Books is an imprint of
Anness Publishing Limited
Hermes House, 88–89 Blackfriars Road,
London SE1 8HA
tel. 020 7401 2077; fax 020 7633 9499
www.lorenzbooks.com; info@anness.com

© Anness Publishing Ltd 2005

UK agent: The Manning Partnership Ltd,
6 The Old Dairy, Melcombe Road, Bath BA2 3LR;
tel. 01225 478 444; fax 01225 478 440;
sales@manning-partnership.co.uk

UK distributor: Grantham Book Services Ltd,
Isaac Newton Way, Alma Park Industrial Estate, Grantham,
Lincs NG31 9SD; tel. 01476 541080; fax 01476 541061;
orders@gbs.tbs-ltd.co.uk

North American agent/distributor: National Book
Network, 4501 Forbes Boulevard, Suite 200, Lanham,
MD 20706; tel. 301 459 3366; fax 301 429 5746;
www.nbnbooks.com

Australian agent/distributor: Pan Macmillan Australia,
Level 18, St Martins Tower, 31 Market St, Sydney,
NSW 2000; tel. 1300 135 113; fax 1300 135 103;
customer.service@macmillan.com.au

New Zealand agent/distributor: David Bateman Ltd,
30 Tarndale Grove, Off Bush Road, Albany, Auckland;
tel. (09) 415 7664; fax (09) 415 8892

A CIP catalogue record for this book is available from
the British Library.

Publisher: *Joanna Lorenz*
Editorial Director: *Helen Sudell*
Senior Editor: *Sarah Ainley*
Designer: *Louise Clements*
Indexer: *Helen Snaith*
Production Controller: *Stephen Lang*

10 9 8 7 6 5 4 3 2 1

contents

introduction

The way in which you surface your garden's pathways, open spaces and sitting areas can have a marked effect on the look and feel of the plot. Different materials and paving designs suggest certain themes and periods in history. Formal paths of antique-style brickwork bring to mind country manor houses, while an expanse of smooth, square paving units creates a distinctly contemporary impression. Garden flooring is often thought of as purely functional, yet there are numerous possibilities for adding creative touches, and even pieces of garden art.

Replacing worn and outdated surfacing materials can transform your garden in much the same way that fitting a new carpet, installing wooden flooring or laying tiling can upgrade a room inside the house. Without spending a great deal of money or causing too much disruption, dull expanses of paving can be renovated by lifting sections and replacing them with other materials to create a more interestingly textured and patterned floor area with colour highlights.

Paving, decking, brickwork and aggregates can all reduce garden maintenance – for example by replacing a lawn or patch of weed-infested ground. Living carpets and lawns act as a foil for border plantings and offer relief from stark hard landscaping. Incorporating dramatic, sweeping curves in your lawn can lift a garden in an instant, and wooden decking is wonderful to walk on barefoot.

Whether your preference is for natural or synthetic materials, traditional or contemporary styling, this book shows you how to plan your garden floor to create desirable features that make the most of problematic surfaces, and how to add character and even a touch of theatre to your garden.

ABOVE: *The selection of flooring materials can have a marked effect on garden atmosphere. Here, a lattice design of bricks and cobbles evokes a pebbly beach.*

OPPOSITE: *Varying the flooring style helps to establish different zones. Here, the smart paved sitting area contrasts well with informal slate shards in the pool garden.*

With a little imagination, your garden floors can be designed from the standpoint of not only practicality but also aesthetics.

How you choose to surface your garden can have a big effect on its overall look and feel. The design potential of floors is all too often overlooked, but there is plenty you can do to introduce shape and form that will add to the experience of exploring the garden.

For example, a simple paving or decking facelift could transform a patio and improve the view from the house; at key points around the garden attractive features can be incorporated into the floor to catch the eye, and materials, colour and pattern can be used to divide the garden into separate zones, creating outdoor rooms for dining or relaxation, or play areas for children.

This section shows how floor treatments can be used to create a change of atmosphere and influence the function of areas in both subtle and dramatic ways.

floor plans

styling & location

As with all aspects of good garden design, the component elements of the floor plan, including lawns, patios and pathways, should blend with the house to form a harmonious picture.

TOP: *A simple deck of smooth, solid timbers is perfect for this contemporary courtyard garden, making the area feel more spacious.*

ABOVE: *Paths of mellow-coloured shingle retained by wooden gravel boards and neat strips of lawn add formality in this traditional garden.*

The interconnecting shapes of lawns, borders, terraces, paths and pools form the 2-D ground plan of the garden – the footprint, if you like, on which the 3-D planting is superimposed. Errors in hard-landscaping are much more difficult to remedy later on, so taking time at the outset for thorough planning is invaluable. The layout of the house, the shape of the plot and any changes in level can guide you to the natural position for individual elements. For example a paved patio may fill in the space created by an L-shaped house extension, while on a steeply sloping site, decking platforms may be an ideal solution to the lack of level ground.

The style of the garden doesn't have to mirror that of the house, although with period properties this is often desirable. However, the materials used for garden floors should fit comfortably with the surrounding buildings and landscape. Don't be afraid to blend traditional and modern ingredients or to mix and match elements, such as bricks, gravel and paving slabs, but exercise restraint by working within a restricted palette. A good approach is to pick up on the materials used in the house construction – for example with a buff brick house, use buff and grey marbled paving slabs with an edging of charcoal grey engineering bricks to match the roof tiles.

In general, the more urban the setting, the more rectilinear the layout can be, with simply designed materials, such as smooth stone, polished wood, ceramic or concrete, arranged as squares and rectangles, decking or poured concrete. Conversely, rural settings benefit from a more relaxed approach with organically shaped sitting areas and curving paths. Floor materials might include cobbles, slate shards, brickwork and irregularly shaped random stone paving. Current design trends are fluid and you can often create a garden that makes reference to more traditional garden styles, such as cottage or seashore, but which is nonetheless contemporary.

RIGHT: *This stylish garden makes full use of the different levels, emphasizing the contrasting areas through the use of hard and soft landscaping elements. This is a large plot and the generous steps are in perfect proportion with the adjoining areas. The stark simplicity of the paving also provides a foil for the exuberant sub-tropical planting. Though this is gardening on a rather grand scale, many of the techniques employed here could be used in a modest suburban plot. Establishing a strong layout or footprint is the key to success.*

Another important factor in creating the right look for your garden floor is scale. Choosing the appropriate size of paving units or surfacing materials is imperative. At one end of the spectrum you might have a tiny corner just big enough to accommodate a café-style table and fold-up chair, and here you could use mini terracotta or granite setts, laid in a circular design. The materials and the decorative design give the sitting area a special feel, making it seem more intimate than if you simply laid a few large concrete paving slabs. At the other end of the scale, consider a period-style property with matching sets of French windows opening on to the garden. Here large, heavy rectangular stone flags create a calm, restful atmosphere, with the paving in proportion to the features of the house and the size of the terrace. Paving the same area in a herringbone pattern of brick could make the space look far too cluttered. Mixing smaller units such as cobbles or setts into a design that is made up of large paviours or using a few large pieces of stone within an area of brickwork can provide a solution for an existing area that has too much of the wrong size of paviour.

Loose materials such as gravel are ideal for pathways and sitting areas in a garden design with lots of free-flowing curves. Most are sufficiently fluid to fill in snaking pathways or undulating patios with curving alcoves hidden among planting. Beach shingle graded towards the edges with rounded pebbles and a few large cobbles will create a seashore feel, while slate shards suggest a Japanese influence. To blend flooring with the vernacular style of the building, try using materials quarried locally. Small modular paving units can also be laid in a way that complements curves; these include bricks, setts and cobbles laid in concrete. A more regular design may be imposed on an irregular shape by way of interlocking and repeat ing elements such as circles. Ones of decreasing size could be used to fit into a tapered area, for example, with the rest of the shape filled in with gravel.

OPPOSITE: *Here, the walls, steps and pathways have been constructed from vernacular materials – locally quarried stone, handmade bricks and beach cobbles – to give an impression of a rustic Italian villa garden.*

TOP: *Random paving set in gravel can produce a soft, relaxed look.*

ABOVE: *Terracotta tiles are the perfect practical and aesthetic choice to surround this gravel "pool".*

Add layers of texture and colour to the fabric of your garden by selecting appropriate paving materials.

a place to sit

Choosing appropriate paving and flooring is key to creating areas set aside for quiet relaxation, entertaining or al fresco dining, and helps to establish the look and feel of an outdoor room.

Eating al fresco is one of the joys of the warm summer months, and being outdoors seems to intensify the senses, making the experience of eating and drinking more sensual. Having a convenient, comfortable place to sit outdoors means you are more likely to get out into the garden, but what happens if you have poorly designed sitting areas?

Newly built houses often have a token "patio" that amounts to little more than a few slabs laid at the back of the house, but this is seldom large enough to accommodate the needs of a family. If the back of the house doesn't get a lot of sun during the day, then other situations should be investigated. A sheltered spot with morning light would be lovely for breakfast or that early morning cup of coffee. Lunch might be best in an eating area under the dappled shade of a climber-clad pergola, and, for people who commute and don't get back home until late, a spot that catches the last few rays might be perfect for a relaxing evening drink or late supper. Tracking the sun's progress around the garden means that you can create sitting areas in all the best locations, allowing you to relocate as necessary. If you prefer to sit in the shade during the hottest part of the day, that would also be something to factor in.

TOP LEFT: *In this backyard the garden takes on the feel of a rustic country kitchen, with the various props and old quarry tiles strengthening the illusion.*

LEFT: *Simple square paving slabs provide a comfortable, level surface for chairs and tables in this all-weather outdoor dining area.*

OPPOSITE: *You don't need to have a patio or terrace to enjoy sitting in the garden. You could set a few bricks or paving stones into a lawn or border to create a firm, dry surface for a chair or bench with just enough space for one or two potted plants.*

A sitting place can be just large enough to accommodate a single chair or bench seat nestling among the plants, or a table and chairs, with space for a couple of steamer chairs perhaps, a barbecue and even an outdoor kitchen or fire pit. Don't forget that you will probably also want space to decorate your outdoor room with pots and planters.

Easy access from the house might be desirable to bring food and drink from the kitchen or to extend the children's play room into the garden; it will also allow for straightforward installation of outdoor lighting. That said, a sitting area out of sight of the house and out of earshot of the phone may be just what you need to get away from it all.

front of house

The front garden is the public face of the property and it should show the house in a positive light. For security reasons, it can be advantageous to have an open space, so that the doorway is in sight of the road.

Gardens at the front of the house should act like entrance halls, instantly making the property welcoming to visitors and sufficiently open to deter burglars who like to operate unseen. A broad horizontal surface emphasises the strong vertical façade of the house and any dramatic architectural plantings.

Make pathways from the street fairly direct to avoid people taking shortcuts over lawns or borders, and give them plenty of room to stand immediately in front of the main door by widening the pathway at this point. This will also allow space for decorative groupings of colourful planters.

The garden space at the front of a property is frequently dominated by vehicles, and where a driveway has been extended to incorporate a turning space or extra parking, the planting tends to be relegated to the margins, which can leave the area looking stark and utilitarian. When there is a need for a large area of hard landscaping that must be able to withstand the weight of a car, thinking ahead about the design allows you to incorporate more attractive features. In modern housing estates, tarmac driveways are often laid as a durable surface, but if you have any input before work begins, try to incorporate at least one sizeable border and find a way to lead the eye towards the front door, perhaps using a path or driveway with a strong, curved line. To prevent tarmac and concrete looking drab, combine it with decorative elements such as brick edging or a border pattern of cobbles or granite setts. Brick paviour driveways are expensive but when laid in different designs, perhaps with a dark brick contrast, they look smart and will raise the value of your property at a stroke.

Front gardens surfaced with gravel or stone chippings are relatively inexpensive and ideal for large areas but they can look untidy without clearly defined boundaries. Containing loose materials with raised brick edging or kerbstone prevents them spilling out on to borders and pathways.

OPPOSITE: *Designing an attractive open area directly in front of the main entrance to a house creates a welcoming ambience. The theme of this contemporary urban space is simplicity, and this has been carried through in the choice of hard landscaping materials.*

TOP: *The front courtyard garden of this property is surfaced with gravel, which creates a soft foil for the architecture and structured planting.*

ABOVE: *Setts are ideal for creating circular features to replace small impractical lawns or to insert into dull stretches of tarmac or concrete.*

playing safe

A large lawn provides a safe and practical area for children's ball games and play equipment.
Other materials, such as play bark and sand, can be put to specific use in smaller areas of the garden.

To avoid too much wear and tear on a lawn, choose a hard-working grass type suitable for your region, such as one containing a high percentage of perennial rye grass (*Lolium perenne*). Aerate worn patches with a garden fork to combat compaction, and irrigate during dry weather to encourage regrowth. Make patch repairs in early autumn or mid-spring. If possible, periodically reposition goal posts and portable play equipment to allow turf to recover. If you don't want to turn the entire lawn into a pitch for ball games, consider separating off one end with a combination of low planting and trellis panels. That way you can keep an eye on the games but still enjoy having a well-maintained lawn for ornamental effect.

Little ones love to pedal toy trucks and tricycles, but for this they need a firm level surface: they get bogged down in gravel and it is an unforgiving surface to fall on. Avoid uneven paving and fence off steps and steep drops to avoid accidents. Surfaces laid with smooth paving units, bricks or concrete are ideal. Consider making a looping "track" around a lawn or central planted area to cut out the need for tricky toddler turns.

There are several types of cushioning play surfaces available although most are too expensive for domestic use. However, beneath a climbing frame you could use a thick layer of play bark (a bark mulch available from garden centres that has no sharp edges or wood chip contamination). There should be few weed problems if it is laid over a landscape membrane.

A sand pit is a great way to occupy young children and may be incorporated into one corner of a paved patio or a wooden deck. The latter makes a useful all-weather play surface if sanded down to remove snags and splinters. In a sunny spot, wood warms up rapidly and dries off quickly after rain. Setting a sand pit into the deck allows you to fit a lid that is flush with the surrounding timber, keeping out cats, rubbish and leaf litter when not in use.

OPPOSITE: *A sheltered sand pit is ideal for little ones, especially one in view of the house. Top up the sand occasionally and then put the cover back in place after use to keep out litter, leaves and cats.*

TOP: *Sown with a hardwearing grass mixture, a lawn makes a great garden floor setting for playing.*

ABOVE: *Smooth paving or decking with a gentle ramp is perfect for pedalling toy trucks and tricycles.*

designing walkways

The path has an important role to play in garden design. Through the use of style and form and the choice of surfacing material, it maps out a floor plan that directs the visitor around the garden.

Traditional advice states that paths should be built so that two persons can walk side by side in comfort. Nowadays, many gardens aren't large enough to accommodate such generous walkways, and you may need to keep the experience of exploring the garden more personal. The style of a path can influence the garden design. Narrow pathways meandering through tall plantings tend to create an atmosphere of suspense and intimacy, while broad, straight walkways generate a formal feel, and when they lead to a strong focal point they may contribute to a theatrical set piece.

The former style may suit a small urban garden where the owners have created a quiet oasis, or a relaxed cottage-style garden. The rigid design of the latter might be found in the garden of a period property or in a large contemporary plot with a rectilinear ground plan.

Whatever kind of pathway you envisage, consider some basic practicalities. One point to watch is that you allow plenty of room for the plants on either side of the path to grow. New pathways of 1m/3ft width might look out of proportion while the planting either side is still young, but rest assured, the situation won't last long. Plants cascading over the edges of paths will soften any hard lines, but if a route is too narrow to start with, you will have to keep cutting back shrubs and perennials to maintain access.

Service pathways are often quite narrow and can be tricky to negotiate with a large wheelbarrow that is top-heavy with garden waste. Ensure that there is space to manoeuvre with no tight corners or awkward bends. Also think about access to all parts of the garden through the year. If your soil is poorly drained, the lawn may become too soggy to walk on in winter but you may still need access to the shed or vegetable plot. In addition, narrow paths and stepping stones that run through deep flower beds allow you to work on either side without treading on the plants.

ABOVE: *In this Japanese-style garden, a pathway of random stepping-stones is set into gravel.*

OPPOSITE: *Screening off parts of a pathway with wooden planks adds an air of mystery and excitement.*

Pathways have the ability to lead the eye, and you can often use the high visibility of a pathway to your advantage. For example with a wide garden that is not very deep, you can fool the onlooker into thinking the garden is bigger by using a curving pathway that tracks the longer, diagonal line. A more formal solution here would be to lay a semi-circular lawn with a pathway following the outer edge of the curve.

Whatever style or design your walkways take, if they come to a full stop, or change direction, give the eye something attractive to focus on. Without this visual reward, you can feel cheated. Path intersections are ideal places for a decorative feature such as a pebble mosaic or a circle composed of bricks, granite setts or specially cut paving slabs.

In a formal garden, such as one having a grid-like ground plan of garden "rooms" divided by one or two main axes, you can add interest to the long, straight pathways by changing the pattern between intersections and widening the pathways at certain key points, incorporating features that will encourage people to pause en route. Constructions along the path that filter the view and prevent you from seeing to the end are ideal; try a rose arbour or a small tree with a circular seat. Other alternatives would be a central pool with a fountain, some kind of sculptural element or a large planter.

Changing the floor surfacing material conveys subtle messages and can make wandering around the garden a more sensual experience. Smooth regular paving and brickwork suggest that you are in a part of the garden that is strongly connected to the house, perhaps more formal and certainly more intensively managed. Random stone paving, perhaps incorporating seashore pebbles, begins to feel more relaxed.

LEFT: *Paving slabs may be shaped to allow you to create modular and flowing designs to suit your plot.*

OPPOSITE, LEFT: *Walkways can be decorative features in their own right when you employ a variety of patterns, colours and textures.*

OPPOSITE, RIGHT: *Loose materials, such as gravel and slate shards or pebbles set in mortar, create a more relaxed atmosphere than paving or brickwork. For practical as well as aesthetic purposes and to create extra definition, try adding stepping stones and random areas of paving.*

To give the suggestion that the garden is becoming more wild or informal, solid paved pathways might give way to shingle edged with wooden gravel boards. You can take this one step further by altering the pathways as you enter certain themed areas. For example a track between a large wildlife pool and a bog garden, or across shingle colonized with seashore plants and grasses, might come in the form of a raised boardwalk of rough timbers. Leaving a cultivated area of lawn and flower borders to enter a mini woodland garden, you could mark the transition point with a simple swing gate and a pathway changing from paving to bark chippings.

living carpets

Lawns are a classic surface material for garden floors but their design potential is rarely exploited in full. Re-shaping a lawn can add impact, while planting fragrant herbs in place of grass adds sensuality.

TOP: *Lawns make smooth open spaces or horizontal voids that create a restful atmosphere in the garden and counterbalance the surrounding jumble of plants.*

ABOVE: *You need a mowing edge to cut edges next to gravel or pebbles.*

OPPOSITE: *This green carpet is a perfect foil for flowers and foliage.*

Lawns provide a verdant foil for flowers and a contrasting horizontal plane for vertical elements such as shrubs, trees and garden structures. In some gardens, lawns flow to fill the space between borders, but in others the lawn is a formal feature, often of rectangular or circular design. Rectangles may have the corners taken off straight or as convex curves. The more defined and ornamental the lawn shape, the more attention it draws, and you should consider whether you have the time or the inclination to maintain it.

Reshaping the lawn can be one of the most effective ways to add design flair to your garden. If you want to move away from straight lines, go for overlapping circles or broad sweeping curves that start and end at logical points, such as the corner of a patio or a specimen tree.

In a long, narrow garden with traditional tramline borders, the eye travels straight to the end, which can make the plot seem dull. Re-shaping the lawn into a broad S-shape will widen the borders in places, enabling strategic planting in the protruding curves – tall specimens that block the view would provide hidden corners to explore and opportunities to add features such as seating alcoves and ornamental structures. A long curving lawn that sweeps diagonally across the garden directs the eye to one corner, and here you could position a single decorative element, such as a raised terrace or deck.

Broad grass walkways make a soft substitute for paving but you may need to add stepping stones for all-weather access. Turf pathways look particularly striking bordered either side by matching flower beds. In areas of the garden where grass turf will not thrive, such as beneath trees, in the shade created by buildings and on very dry soil, use plants that will cope with the conditions. In a modern landscape, areas of evergreen ground cover look effective contrasting with paving or formal pools, creating a simple, low-maintenance ground pattern.

stepping stones

You may not want to lay a full-scale pathway in planted areas of the garden or to track across a lawn. Here, stepping stones make an ideal compromise. Choose a design that suits the surroundings.

In formal gardens, pre-cast concrete paving slabs can be laid into grass. Squares work well as a regular pattern, such as a line of diamonds, and circles can be laid in a gentle arc. To protect an overused area of lawn or to create a contemporary effect in gravel, try a broad swathe of square or rectangular paving laid with small gaps in between. For a naturalistic feel, use randomly sized pieces of split stone such as slate or sandstone. Stepping stones are great fun for children, especially if you use designs with animal and bird imprints or fairytale characters.

Before setting the pieces into the ground, lay them out to check you are happy with the pattern and that you can walk comfortably from one stone to another. In lawns, lay stones slightly below the grass surface, so that the mower passes over them without damaging the blades. Turf will eventually spread across the stones, but it can be cut back with a strimmer.

Stepping stones laid in gravel are a familiar design element in Japanese Zen gardens. Traditional arrangements have names that describe the pattern, such as "ganko", which translates as "wild geese", and "chidori", which means "zigzag". Granite is a popular material, but porous rock such as limestone, which becomes colonized with mosses and algae, will also work very well. Path intersections are marked by a single large stone that encourages you to pause before deciding which route to take.

In a Mediterranean-style gravel garden, a natural stepping stone pathway can make an attractive feature as well as providing access. Stagger large, wide pieces of stone or reclaimed timber, setting them close together to make a track.

TOP LEFT: *Timber makes a textured pathway through shingle.*

LEFT: *Round stones continue the circular theme of this garden.*

OPPOSITE: *Stepping stones work well in more relaxed parts of the garden, providing all-weather access. Here, the stones disappear behind a tree to create a sense of mystery.*

changing levels

Well-proportioned steps are an eye-catching design feature, and even a small incline could be capitalized on by introducing one or two steps in a sloping pathway or between a raised terrace and a lawn.

Broad, shallow steps can look stunning in a garden setting and are easily and safely negotiated by children and adults alike. Avoid making steps designed for a mountain goat unless there is a stout handrail; on a very steeply sloping garden construct your pathways so that they zigzag diagonally across the plot, making the climb more manageable. Steps are usually thought of as rectangular and moving in a straight line, but there are numerous interesting variations. For example, you could create curved steps coming off a circular terrace or lawn, or a fan of wedge-shaped steps to accommodate a change in direction or to create a grand double staircase.

In a traditional setting, steps can be made from solid pieces of stone or from brickwork. In a contemporary garden, steps can look very effective in concrete. This is poured into moulds created from wooden shuttering or breeze blocks. Concrete is a very versatile material and can also be used to create steps with crisp, geometric curves. To add decorative detail, plain concrete treads could be edged with brick or with vertical stone pieces sandwiched together with cement, like wafers. For a Spanish-style look, you could decorate the treads with patterns composed of pebbles or shards of slate, perhaps mixing in colourful strips of ceramic tile.

Rustic steps might be built from rough stone blocks or stout timber risers back-filled with hardcore topped with gravel, stone chippings or slate shards. The latter is one of the least expensive ways to landscape a slope and there are a number of variations. On a gentle incline, the edges of the steps can be made with 2.5cm/1in thick talanized gravel board, and the risers from wooden sleepers. Alternatively, use stout posts of circular cross-section held in place with wooden pegs. For steeper steps, set the posts end-on in concrete. Wooden steps work particularly well in a shaded garden planted with ferns, with the treads surfaced with tree bark.

OPPOSITE, TOP: *Steps can be built as features that fit a style of garden. Here, pieces of slate forming the risers add a rustic note.*

OPPOSITE, BOTTOM: *Crisp concrete retaining walls and steps topped with smooth slabs are ideal for creating a minimalist look in city gardens.*

RIGHT: *Wooden decking platforms are a stylish and practical way to deal with changes in floor level.*

BELOW: *Slabs of roughly hewn stone create access up a steep woodland bank.*

A sloping garden is generally regarded as a problem site but it affords numerous opportunities for imaginative landscaping. Steep gardens may need extensive building work to create the necessary levels, or a skilled decking company to superimpose a series of secure wooden platforms over the slope, but when the work is complete you will have a useable, practical garden space, plus a whole new – and completely unique – dimension to your property.

A house that is situated at the top of a hill can have a commanding position with fine views over the garden and surrounding landscape, but the lack of privacy is always a potential downside and adequate structures will need to be constructed to shelter the sitting area. When a property is at the bottom of a slope, there can be problems with surface drainage and a lack of light near the house. Here it makes sense to build sitting areas towards the top of the garden, to make the most of the view from the elevated position.

The creation of a flat, open space by excavating land next to the house may require the construction of a retaining wall to hold back the soil. For safety reasons this is most definitely a job for professional contractors. However, rather than have one high wall, consider building a series of shallow terraces. That way, the patio won't feel quite so hemmed in. If a substantial retaining wall is your only option, introduce a wide gap in the wall using steps that are lined up with French windows or a patio door to help open up the garden from the terrace and make it feel more welcoming. Building the retaining wall so that it curves gently or is stepped will also help to soften the impact.

OPPOSITE: *Here, a rill and mini waterfall, which flows into a hidden reservoir where the water is re-circulated, are used to make a feature of the terracing.*

ABOVE LEFT: *Building a retaining wall has enabled the creation of a sizeable terrace with a flight of steps to connect the two levels.*

ABOVE RIGHT: *A stepped wall used to emphasize a sloping garden.*

Pathways that ascend or descend through a series of terraces will look far more interesting if they incorporate a number of twists and turns with fan-shaped steps, or flights set at right angles to one another. To make flowing, irregularly shaped steps with a rounded or organic profile in areas that are likely to have relatively light foot traffic, first mould and compact the ground, working hardcore into the soil, and make the approximate shape of the steps using pieces of broken brick or breeze block. Cover with a stiff cement mixture containing plasticizer to allow you to sculpt the concrete into smooth curves before it sets. Scatter small pebbles or gravel on to the wet concrete of the tread for texture and extra grip.

One contemporary way to landscape a shallow slope or to join an upper and lower terrace is to use stepped walls of rendered breeze blocks or poured concrete, which will also provide impromptu seating. Decking platforms supported by stout piers and joists, and which are connected by flights of open steps, can also provide a relatively inexpensive way of creating level sitting areas in different parts of a sloping garden. A cantilevered deck can even make an outdoor space adjacent to a house that is perched at the top of a steep slope.

edge effects

There are aesthetic as well as practical reasons for edging paths, driveways, terraces and lawns. Not only can a band of bricks set in a bed of mortar reduce the need for trimming the edges of a lawn, it can also provide an attractive frame, raising the profile of the area by defining the lawn shape more crisply.

A raised edging is necessary to contain loose materials such as gravel or stone chippings, preventing soil from spilling over from the borders and reducing problems with weed growth. The nature of the edging material strongly influences the overall feel of the garden. Bricks or kerbstones with mortared joints give a neat finish that is suitable for contemporary and period gardens alike. By contrast, rough stone blocks or logs laid end-to-end with the bark intact have a more relaxed, organic feel. Log roll made from split logs wired together can be used to edge curves, the material being nailed on to stout wooden pegs. For a more substantial looking and durable solution that is more fitted to a modern town garden or Japanese-style landscape, use lengths of stripped logs treated with non-toxic preservative and set end-on into a bed of mortar so that the tops are flush with one another.

If you want to add a decorative finishing touch to a plain pathway or paved area, choose an option that enhances the existing design or theme – for example a simple repeating pattern of pebbles set in mortar or a ceramic mosaic could create an attractive border for a Mediterranean-style terrace.

Brick edging works very well for many kinds of paving, and the bricks can be laid in a number of ways for creative effects. In a cottage garden you could set the bricks diagonally into a bed of mortar to give a jagged raised edging. To provide a narrow strip of colour flush with the existing paving you can add one or more rows of bricks laid flat and end-to-end.

If you prefer a slightly softer, more relaxed feel for your garden, try a border of two or three rows of granite setts instead of brickwork. Cobbles and setts can also be laid proud of the surrounding surface to make the design more prominent. To divert foot traffic away from certain areas while still maintaining an attractive low-maintenance surface, use raised cobbles and setts to create broad swathes on one or both sides of the main route.

OPPOSITE: *The dry stone walling used here to separate the lawned areas from the pathway is perfectly in keeping with the slate material used for the path. Notice how the edging has been tapered to give emphasis to the undulations.*

TOP: *Timber with a non-toxic preservative is ideal for raised vegetable beds, separating soil from gravel paths.*

ABOVE: *A brick mowing strip makes a decorative border for the lawn and reduces edging work.*

pattern

Using a variety of materials, you can create one-off elements within paving or borders, utilizing repeated patterns to add decoration and individuality to the floor without having to resurface the entire area.

Small, modular paving units, such as engineering bricks, granite setts or tiles, are perfect for creating patterns for the garden floor. There are a number of traditional arrangements for bricks, including herringbone and basket weave, and circular designs are possible by making the mortar joints wedge-shaped. There is even more flexibility with square setts, ranging from grid patterns to swirling spirals. Pebbles, too, offer endless possibilities. Like cobbles, they are sold by size and colour, making preparation simple. Work to a scale drawing and lay the design out before fixing it in mortar.

In a terrace that is overlooked by the house, pattern can be incorporated into paving to make an eye-catching feature. Square or rectangular areas are relatively straightforward and can be laid out to look like a Persian rug. Try creating a broad, multi-layered border using bricks, setts, pebbles, square paving slabs or tiles, taking care to link the materials used to the house or other paved areas of the garden. To prevent the area looking overly fussy, the bulk of the terrace could then be filled in with plain tiling or paving slabs. If you use square pieces, set them on the diagonal; this requires more cutting but will give a more dynamic design. Leave room at the centre for a mosaic panel of pebbles or slate shards, a jewel-like insert of colourful ceramic tiles or a small fountain.

For a striking alternative, lay out a chequerboard design of light and dark paving squares, alternating slate with Indian sandstone or black and terracotta coloured ceramic tiles. On a smaller scale, create patterned paving features around a garden seat set into a border or alcove, to edge a formal pool or to mark the junction of pathways. For the latter, a circular element incorporating a compass motif made of mosaic would be particularly pertinent.

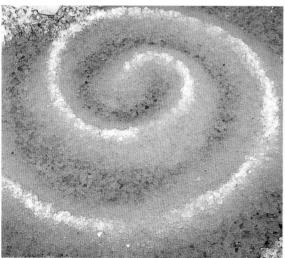

ABOVE LEFT: *A simply designed pebble mosaic is not hard to construct using differently coloured pebbles and stone shards.*

LEFT: *This swirling pattern is made from recycled glass chips and is reminiscent of glacial ice. Glass beads can also be added to mosaics.*

ABOVE: *The stark contrast in the chequerboard floor design makes this outdoor room, with its clipped topiary, seem all the more dramatic.*

RIGHT: *A zebra-inspired pattern has been created using a clever mix of coloured pebbles to give a contemporary mosaic effect.*

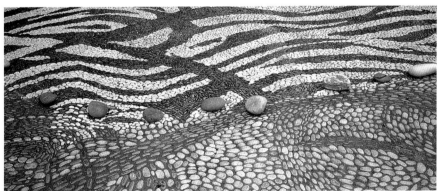

flooring facelift

One of the main reasons why garden floors are often ignored is the cost of resurfacing such a large area. With clever use of materials, however, you can add enough interest to lift tired or dilapidated flooring.

Replacing driveways and large areas of outdoor flooring can be a costly proposition but there are ways to upgrade patios and pathways for relatively little outlay. Cleaning up old stone and concrete paving to remove dirt and algae can work wonders for a jaded patio. Hire a heavy-duty pressure washer for the day and use a proprietary patio-cleaning solution for problem areas following the manufacturer's instructions.

Large concrete paving slabs laid in a regular pattern of squares or rectangles can be very monotonous, especially when used to cover substantial areas. A facelift can be simple to effect, however. One approach is to lift the paving slabs of a terrace – some in random clusters and some in single units – and to replace them with ground-cover planting, such as a block of identical ornamental grasses, loose cobbles laid over landscape membrane or a combination of the two. When planting, dig out the sand and hardcore and replace with good quality top soil. Alternatively, fill spaces with shingle or small pebbles, or with infills of modular paving units such as bricks, setts or cobbles laid on a base of sand and mortar. If you are replacing paving units along a pathway with panels of cobbles laid in a pattern, lift the paving slabs from the edges and alternate them diagonally so that the pathway continues to wind comfortably between the uneven surfaces.

Expanses of concrete or tarmac are harder to deal with, but with the help of professional contractors you can still improve their appearance. Specialist cutting tools can be used to create a sharp, vertical edge, allowing you to add a decorative margin, incorporating planting or stones.

Gravel drives can be problematic as the surface wears thin over time, and without a well-defined margin it is hard to keep the area looking neat. Adding an edging appropriate to the garden style is well worth the investment. Redistribute uneven gravel with a rake; if extra depth is needed, cover the entire area with a matching material – applying it in patches will only highlight the difference between the old, weathered material and the new.

OPPOSITE: *Instead of using one single flooring element, different materials have been used to break up the open space of this large courtyard area, creating subtle patterns and changes in texture and colouring.*

TOP: *Use paving circles and setts laid in contrasting patterns to add interest within areas of stone chippings or gravel.*

ABOVE: *Scrap metal stampings make an unusual and striking filler.*

One way to inject an element of style into mundane garden flooring is to add inserts of a luxury material. A good example would be a patio garden paved with square slabs of concrete. By removing some of the slabs at random and cutting them in half to give smaller rectangular slabs, you can create a jigsaw-type layout with irregular gaps, which can then be filled with high-quality decorative elements: you might use brightly glazed ceramic tiles; inserts of pebble mosaic or ceramic tesserae; pieces of polished marble or slate; or antique bricks or granite setts laid in small blocks. To add textural variation, try using pieces of split stone or slate laid on edge. One contemporary idea would be to insert blue-green or clear glass bricks fitted with a halogen light to shine up through the paving at night.

To break the monotony of a large terrace or long, straight pathway, pave it in one type of material, such as paving slabs or poured concrete, but first split the area into large panels, using contrasting bands of brickwork, coloured tiles, setts or pebbles to frame each section. Every now and then, one of these squares or rectangles could contain a decorative panel. Think hard before ripping up an area of paving and starting entirely from scratch. The slabs could be cleaned up and re-laid, and this may be enough to update the whole area.

Irregularly shaped patios often leave awkward corners to fill, and rather than trying to cut smaller pieces of paving to fit, it can look better and will be quicker and less costly to use gravel or glass chippings, or shards of glazed tiles set in mortar. Large square or rectangular areas fully paved with slabs can also be made more interesting by lifting units from the edge to create irregular but flowing shapes, the margins filled in as described. To relieve a similarly monotonous tract of gravel, consider grading the material towards the edges, using waves of increasingly larger pebbles, cobbles and rounded boulders to create the effect of a shingle beach or mountain stream. You might even insert a fan or stepped arrangement of weathered railway sleepers (ties), but not near anything edible, because of the chemicals they contain.

TOP: *Bordering a small pond with sand, beach pebbles and reclaimed wood creates a fresh seashore look.*

ABOVE: *An arresting juxtaposition of clipped box balls set on blue acrylic chips forms a striking grid.*

OPPOSITE: *One dramatic way of facelifting a formerly dull area of paving is to incorporate a water feature. At the centre of this snail-shell paving design is a glazed ceramic fountain which feeds into a concealed reservoir.*

There is now an ever-increasing choice of materials available for use on floor surfaces, with many products being designed with the do-it-yourself enthusiast in mind.

Paving slabs are now being made smaller and lighter for easy handling, and materials such as brick paviours and setts are widely available to the amateur gardener. Though the fashion in decking comes and goes, you will find all the necessary materials on hand to build a smart-looking deck in a weekend.

This section considers where best to use hard-landscaping materials around the garden, outlining the pros and cons of each, and giving expert hints and tips on how to lay and maintain them. There is advice on sourcing materials and saving money by using cheaper substitutes that look almost as good as original stone, brick or granite. Finally, there is a look at different approaches to lawn maintenance and ideas for original ways of creating living carpets.

materials

stone

Natural stone is the crème de la crème of paving materials and usually the most expensive. With its uneven surface and variable colouring, it works well in almost any style of garden.

Top: *Slate contrasts with Indian sandstone in this smart terrace.*

Above: *Stone is effective in both modern and traditional settings.*

Opposite: *Stone mellows beautifully with age. Here, uneven paving and plants seeded into the crevices of the stonework add to the charm of this country garden.*

Sandstone and limestone are popular because the stone can be split into flat pieces, and will soon develop an attractive weathered patina through colonization by algae, lichens and mosses. Reclaimed paving can be found in architectural salvage yards and stone merchants but tends to be costly and may be available only in a limited size range, such as large rectangular slabs, which are heavy and difficult to manoeuvre. However, you can now buy imported Indian sandstone, which substitutes nicely for antique stone paving and can work out only a little more expensive than the best quality concrete paviours. It can be cut to a variety of sizes, allowing for random paving, and is available in subtle shade variations, with beautiful colour veining showing up when wet.

Some types of stone will complement both contemporary and period properties. Slate paving, which glistens after rain, is a fine example, and as well as being laid on its own can also be used to create panels surrounded by bricks or granite setts. Granite is the most hardwearing form of stone, but the cost makes it most suited to areas of detail. Likewise, marble is something of a luxury element and polished pieces may be used for occasional highlights.

Lay stone slabs on consolidated hardcore topped with raked coarse sand or hoggin. Large, thick stone slabs may be laid directly on to the sand, but in most cases, in order to keep the slabs firm and steady on ground that has minor undulations, blobs of cement are used. These allow for easy adjustments to be made before it has set. Using a firm mix of five or six parts sand to one of cement, put dollops on the ground near each corner and one in the middle and then lower the slab on top. Gently tamp down, checking frequently with a straight-edge and spirit-level that the surface is even with an appropriate fall for drainage. Do not walk on the slabs until the mixture has hardened.

wood

Flooring made from wood, with its subtle tones and grain patterns, has a timeless, natural appeal.
Wood weathers attractively with the elements but it can also be coloured with stains and paints.

A few tree species are rich in protective resins, most notably Western red cedar. These have a natural resistance to rot and shouldn't require any chemical preservative treatment, though they will benefit aesthetically from the application of wood oil. The same goes for hardwoods, whose durability stems from their dense grain structure. Temperate hardwoods used for decking include oak and ash; tropical hardwoods include iroko, ipe, tatajuba, yellowood and cumaru. Less durable softwoods include Southern yellow pine and the least expensive wood, Scandinavian pine. Softwoods are normally pressure-treated with preservative, which takes the chemicals right the way through the planks. Despite assurances about the sustainability of "cropping" tropical hardwoods, there are concerns about the impact on existing forest ecosystems. Using reclaimed timber or timber from managed plantations in cool temperate regions is a more eco-friendly option.

Timber can be laid in a variety of ways to create different effects. Raw, reclaimed timber such as railway sleepers (ties) that are impregnated with tar may be set directly on to a hardcore base to provide a rugged-looking walkway; sleepers can also be spaced farther apart to create textural contrast within an expanse of gravel. These and other similarly chunky timbers may be used to create a bridge over a stream, as well as to build steps and terraces.

Broad, smooth reclaimed wooden planks work well for large areas of decking, the timber having a worn, ready-aged appearance that works well with period, country garden or seaside properties. Plain, wide planks are also better for building decked floors in a contemporary or minimalist setting such as an urban roof terrace.

Creating patterns in decked areas can be straightforward provided you have basic woodworking skills. One idea is to vary the angle at which the planks are laid.

ABOVE: *Weight restrictions for balconies and roof terraces can often be overcome by suspending a decked floor from joists fixed to the walls. This then allows for the creation of a transformed garden floor in wood.*

TOP: *The pattern of parallel lines created by plain wooden decking suits minimalist garden designs.*

OPPOSITE: *A raised deck lies at an angle to the paving, creating an informal atmosphere.*

Ensure that decking planks have been properly seasoned or dried out and that they have been stored under cover before they are laid. Otherwise the wood may shrink, crack and warp as it dries. The thicker the wood, the less likely it is to bend: 2cm/^{3}/4in is common for cheaper, softwood decking planks, but 2.5cm/1in is better. Lay over timber joists raised up on concrete piers to keep them away from the damp ground. Provided the wood has good air circulation and is not in direct contact with the ground, it should be resistant to rotting. Cover the ground beneath the deck with semi-permeable landscape membrane to prevent weeds growing up between the planks.

Decking planks often have a scored surface to give a better grip underfoot, although this can mar the look of the wood. While it may not be necessary in dry climates or in a sun-drenched spot, it can be useful in shady or damp areas where algae tend to colonize, creating a dangerously slippery surface. Clean off algal build-up twice a year using a pressure sprayer, and consider tacking galvanized wire mesh on to the planks to provide a non-slip surface; even if you prefer not to use mesh on the deck area for aesthetic reasons, you could fix it to wooden access steps as a safety measure.

ABOVE LEFT: *A raised wooden boardwalk adds authenticity to a seaside garden.*

ABOVE RIGHT: *Wood is relatively easy to manipulate into more angular and adventurous designs.*

OPPOSITE: *A shelter like this can be built quite cheaply using fencing materials and reclaimed timber. Treatment against rotting is advised.*

Treating the decking with yacht varnish, coloured stains and decking paints is known as re-finishing. Remove snags and splinters with a utility knife and sand the deck smooth with a sanding block in the direction of the grain. Sanding encourages the surface to absorb stains and decking treatments more easily.

Waterproof lighting units can be installed flush with a deck floor and these are tough enough to walk on. Position lights at exit and entry points, to illuminate steps and changes in level. On a more decorative note, why not install coloured optical fibre elements? These are fitted through tiny drilled holes, sparkling magically at night. The wiring can be safely tucked away out of sight; this is also a plus point for built-in water features, since you can hide the pump and reservoir.

As a natural material, wood blends effortlessly with the surrounding plants and weathers to create a subtle patina.

ABOVE: *Concrete is not just for stark urban landscapes. Here, broad, gently curving steps of a muted grey provide a pleasing line and blend beautifully with the adjacent grasses.*

LEFT: *Tinted concrete provides both a platform for seating and a raised pool in this restful modern garden. Notice how the rounded boulder, curved seats and planting soften the straight lines.*

concrete

One of the most versatile and potentially inexpensive materials for surfacing the garden is concrete which can be plain grey or colour tinted, textured or imprinted.

Square or rectangular blocks of smooth concrete paving are created by filling an area enclosed by wooden shuttering, which is later removed. Ensure that the base is properly prepared and well compacted with a good depth of hardcore, otherwise the concrete will crack when walked on or driven over. Tamp down the mixture with a screeding plank to drive out air bubbles and ensure an even surface.

Geometrically shaped concrete sections work well in a contemporary setting combined with areas of lawn, deck or some form of loose material. The technique of shuttering can also be adapted to create concrete steps and terraces. Meanwhile, straight or curving concrete paths can be made by filling in between brick edging strips or treated gravel board held in place with pegs. Texture smooth concrete before it sets, using a straight-edge such as a plank of wood for a ridged effect, or a nylon bristle hand brush dipped in a bucket of water for softer swirls and stipples.

You can also lay concrete in fluid, organic shapes, perhaps contained by dry-stone walling for a rustic look. To create an interesting weathered appearance, say in a cottage or seaside garden, work pea shingle and cobbles into the surface of the concrete before it dries and use a fine water spray and soft brush to expose pieces of the stone. You might also add coloured glass beads or pieces of glazed ceramic tile by hand.

Specialist driveway and patio contractors can create the look of bricks, slate tiles, block paving or granite setts and even wooden planks with the aid of templates. These imprint patterns into a coloured surface layer that overlays the raw concrete base. The surface can also be given an antique look to give the illusion of weathered brick or stone. Afterwards, the concrete is sealed to help protect it from erosion. Concrete colourants are available to tint concrete as it is being mixed; you can even paint concrete afterwards, which is less durable.

TOP: *Sections of pre-cast concrete punctuate this gravel path, creating textural interest. Concrete sleepers imprinted with a wood-grain pattern are surprisingly convincing.*

ABOVE: *Small square paving slabs can create a surface similar to indoor floor tiles, adding to the room-like quality of a garden area while providing a foil for greenery.*

paving

Concrete paving slabs have come a long way since the first plain grey, pink or buff-coloured offerings.
Not only has the colour range expanded, but so too has the number of different textures and finishes.

Circular paving features for use on their own or within larger terraces, and slabs that are surfaced to look like stable-block paving or setts, are just some of the variations you will find in garden centres and builder's merchants.

Riven slabs with an undulating surface similar to split sandstone or limestone, and with subtle mottling, vary in quality, but at a glance you would be hard-pressed to tell the difference between a better quality concrete reproduction and natural stone. Stone-effect paving works particularly well laid randomly using a combination of squares and rectangles. Square units may start as small as 30cm/12in, but 45cm/18in and 60cm/24in slabs are the most common. If rectangular elements are not available in your chosen range, it would be worth hiring a diamond cutter to cut some 60cm/24in slabs in half. Another way to add a rustic feel to this type of random flooring is to work in occasional groupings of engineering bricks or antique-style block paviours in twos and threes.

Identical plain, square paving slabs with crisp edges work well in contemporary and minimalist settings. For most circumstances, choose the 45cm/18in size, which will be in scale with typical domestic garden settings. Another plus point is that these slabs are relatively easy to handle on your own, lessening the risk of back injury. To add a more dynamic touch, lay the slabs on the diagonal, using a taut line for referencing the position of the first row of slabs.

You can now buy slabs that look like handmade terracotta floor tiles – perfect for a Mediterranean-style terraced garden. Take care with speciality paviours, since there is a possibility that strong sunlight and general wear and tear will cause fading. Accidental damage can also reveal the concrete interior, spoiling the illusion. It is worth consulting the manufacturers directly for advice on this matter, including tips on how best to preserve the surface.

OPPOSITE: *In this stylish terrace, the designer has taken advantage of the open space to introduce a bold geometric design, using dark-coloured paving units. In a smaller area, choose paving elements that are to the scale of the plot.*

TOP RIGHT: *Square reconstituted stone tiles combine with lush sub-tropical plants to suggest a Moorish influence.*

RIGHT: *Smooth grey paving slabs and rendered walls combine to give a smart, contemporary flavour.*

setts & paviours

Manufacturers now offer a wide range of hardwearing paving units, including those that look like antique bricks or granite setts, the latter being less expensive than the original and easier to source.

Concrete paviours (or setts – the words are interchangeable) may be interlocking, fitting together like a jigsaw puzzle and producing a contemporary effect, but squares and rectangles are the most versatile. Those with rounded edges or a domed profile tend to produce a softer, more old-fashioned look.

Visit the displays of paving specialists and builder's merchants to see how the units you are interested in will look when laid. Take time to decide what effect will best suit your project in terms of the scale of paving unit used and the style, and don't forget that you can mix different materials and colours to provide interest over larger areas. Plain concrete paviours would be ideal for the front driveway of a contemporary-style building, perhaps edged in a contrasting colour, while traditional materials, such as granite setts or a good concrete reproduction, would suit a circular terrace in the garden of a period property.

Concrete colours range from buff-yellow to red, pink and terracotta shades, as well as greys and charcoal. In addition, the surface texture and mottling give an age-worn feel to the paviour. However, in areas of heavy use, the surface colouring may wear – something that doesn't happen with clay paviours.

Purpose-made setts and paviours are popular for surfacing driveways, but smaller units can be laid in a number of designs and patterns around the garden. More expensive elements, such as granite or hand-made terracotta setts, are ideal for edging effects and occasional detailing to add decoration or upgrade low-budget paving.

The depth of foundation depends on the type of soil and the amount of wear and tear expected, but you will need well-consolidated hardcore, 75–100mm/3–4in deep, topped with 35–50mm/1^1/2–2in of coarse grit sand as a base. Fill the joints with dry silica sand. Brush off the surface and use a vibrating plate compactor to settle the units in position.

OPPOSITE: *Brick paviours can be used to add colour and interest to large areas of stone or concrete paving, creating eye-catching designs or adding small decorative touches. There are a number of classic patterns that can be tried.*

RIGHT: *Here, sections of paving have been laid using contrasting materials laid at varying angles. Notice how the central portion is contained with an edging strip, and how the curving side cuts into an area of square setts.*

Bricks are relatively lightweight and easy to handle. Like concrete block paviours, they are laid on a bed of sand over consolidated hardcore, which means that you have time to experiment with their positioning and complex patterns can be laid with the aid of a brick cutter (block splitter).

A containing edging is used to hold the bricks in position and is usually made from bricks or setts fixed into concrete. Engineering bricks are typically used to edge driveways and terraces. Unlike most modern house bricks, they are flat on both sides, smooth-textured and impervious to moisture. Moisture resistance and density is essential in a brick chosen for garden flooring because if water penetrates the surface in winter it can freeze, causing flaking and disintegration. House bricks are unsuitable, and you must be careful to check that reclaimed or "antique" bricks are of the required quality.

For large projects, you may need more than one pallet or pack of bricks. Have them delivered at the same time so that you can use bricks from the different pallets simultaneously, otherwise subtle variations in colouring can create patches. For an interesting textured look, combine several different brick types, perhaps dotting a few darker or brindled bricks into a lighter mix. You can also use bricks and setts in combination with larger stone or concrete slabs, or with loose aggregates. Clay bricks can be slightly imperfect in terms of size and shape, which adds character.

With paths and patios involving designs such as basket weave or herringbone, start from a point where you can use whole bricks and come back later to fill in the gaps, being careful not to tread on the completed sections. For designs

ABOVE: *Here, old bricks have been laid in a circular pattern at a path intersection for decorative interest. Low box hedging neatly frames the design.*

OPPOSITE: *In a garden, brick flooring can create a mellow country or cottage garden feel, especially when planting flows over the path edges.*

BELOW: *Due to the cost of traditional granite setts, they are often confined to creating attractive highlights and edging for other types of paving.*

starting from a straight or diagonal line, use a piece of taut string as a reference point. As with block paviours, fill in gaps in brick paving with dry silica sand and consolidate. Ensure that the finished paving has an even surface with a steady fall, away from buildings if possible, so that water drains properly and doesn't lie in pools. Extra drainage provision may also be necessary to divert large volumes of rainfall efficiently.

pebbles & cobbles

The smooth, rounded shapes of pebbles, cobbles and boulders are particularly pleasing to the eye, and when they are wet their surfaces gleam, revealing previously hidden colours and mottling.

Small pebbles can be purchased in bags of different sizes and are effective for landscaping large areas if they are combined with similarly coloured gravels or larger cobbles and boulders in overlapping bands. You might try this effect next to a pool lined with butyl rubber, continuing the pebbles under water to camouflage the shelving margin. Alternatively, call to mind a mountain stream by contouring the ground and creating a dry river bed of pebbles, cobbles and boulders. For a natural effect, settle the larger stones into the surrounding pebbles rather than placing them on the surface. To complete the illusion, cross the "stream" with a simple wooden bridge – a technique seen in Japanese dry-garden landscapes known as *karesansui*.

A seaside feel could be conjured up using reclaimed timber to create a raised boardwalk over cobbles and pebbles, with blue-green grasses, sedges and silver-leaved sea buckthorn (*Hippophae rhamnoides*) used to imitate salt-tolerant vegetation. You might even add a beach hut-style tool shed and props such as fishing nets and glass floats, as well as a stripy deckchair.

Cobbles are great fillers for large, awkward gaps created when rectilinear shaped terraces and decks are laid on a diagonal relative to the property. They also work well in contemporary settings, especially when combined with the smooth surfaces of modern decking, square paving slabs or concrete. In addition, cobbles can be used as a decorative mulch for strong architectural plants or to cover the ground around a specimen tree. Lay loose cobbles and pebbles over landscape membrane to prevent weeds coming through.

The rounded texture of cobbles makes them difficult to walk on unless well bedded into concrete, but this can be turned to your advantage if you want to create no-go areas, such as on either side of the main thoroughfare in a front garden. Avoid using loose cobbles in areas that collect litter or autumn leaves as this sort of material is difficult to brush out.

ABOVE: *By utilizing different colours and sizes of pebbles you can create attractive original ground-cover patterns, such as this spiral.*

OPPOSITE: *Smooth flat stones are ideal for paths through lawns that don't have an edging strip.*

RIGHT: *A wooden bridge crosses a stream with a beach of pebbles and cobbles merging into shingle.*

FAR RIGHT: *Flattened beach shingle forms a very eye-catching path floor.*

terracotta & ceramic

The illusion of an outdoor room is greatly enhanced by covering the floor with ceramic tiles. Depending on the tile style, the effect can be contemporary, rustic, or suggestive of a particular country or culture.

Quarry tiles are relatively inexpensive and when laid over a broad floor space they bring to mind a farmhouse kitchen or simple, Mediterranean-style al fresco living, especially if the surrounding walls are whitewashed. Quarry tiles are quite often associated with Victorian and Edwardian houses, where they were typically used to create pathways leading to the front door. In this case, as well as the familiar red-brown tiles you might see ones patterned with black and cream motifs, which were sometimes used as a decorative margin with the interior tiles set on the diagonal. You can purchase reclaimed quarry tiles in plain and patterned designs from architectural salvage yards; don't worry about mixing the designs, as any differences in appearance will add an old-fashioned charm.

Flooring specialists offer ceramic tiles suitable for use indoors and out, so check before you buy that your selection is frostproof and relatively non-slip when wet. It is sometimes safer to use natural stone tiles such as versatile slate or pale limestone, without a polished or glazed surface. The latter works particularly well in modern urban settings with glass and metal surrounds but may chip.

Large, square floor tiles in soft terracotta or buff shades tend to suggest a hot climate, and you can emphasize this by dressing the "set" with props and plants appropriate to a favourite region or culture to build up a theme. To add a relaxed Mexican or Californian flavour to your patio or terrace, you might try adding cacti, yuccas and agaves; to suggest hot and sultry Morocco, perhaps add shiny metal containers with tropical foliage plants such as palms and banana trees; while to capture the sensuality of a Tuscan villa in your backyard, you could install a bubbling wall fountain and add fragrant citrus trees, oleander and bay topiary in giant terracotta pots, with overhead shade provided by a pergola woven with grape vines.

To add dramatic impact to a large square or rectangular terrace, why not create a Persian-carpet effect, adding colour to plain terracotta flooring by laying a border of rich blue glazed tiles and inserting a central panel of highly decorative Moorish tiles. Alternatively, individual patterned tiles could be used in a more informal way, set randomly and widely spaced into a plain concrete paved surface, where the brightly coloured glazes would make them stand out like jewels. Another contemporary idea is to use colourful tile fragments to create flowing, abstract mosaic patterns. Ceramic shards also work well with pebbles, adding vibrancy to mosaic panels.

OPPOSITE: *Small glazed terracotta tiles, more commonly known as quarry tiles, are ideal for paving tiny backyard gardens as well as balconies and roof-top terraces. They are relatively lightweight compared to standard paving slabs or bricks, and are impervious to the elements. In addition, the colouring is a warm earth tone, which is perfect for complementing garden greenery.*

ABOVE: *Colourful, intricately patterned ceramic tiles and mosaic panels are a feature of Moorish-influenced gardens. Plain glazed tiles in rich colours such as ultramarine can also be used to add occasional highlights within a paved area.*

gravel & chippings

The water-worn surface and subtle colouring of river gravel and beach shingle create a soft, natural look, while synthetic alternatives add drama. Both offer a solution for small or unusually shaped areas.

Gravel is graded by the size of individual pieces and it is important to choose the right type. If it is too fine, the fragments will be kicked around, creating worn patches, and they will get stuck in the tread of your shoes. A 2cm/³⁄4in diameter is ideal for surfacing a patio, pathway or drive because the pieces bed down into a hardcore base and will stabilize once they have been walked over a few times.

Gravel is ideal in an informal country or seaside garden with meandering pathways, or as a low-maintenance surface between the beds of a formal potager. In a contemporary setting, too, gravel works well flowing into awkward spaces and providing a contrasting texture with modern decking or areas paved with concrete slabs. Gravel can also be used as a mulch around plants, and looks especially effective with succulents and architectural foliage plants.

In this case, a semi-permeable membrane or landscape fabric is laid to prevent weed growth. Cut crosses with a modelling knife, plant through these holes, and cover with gravel. If such an area is walked over, the gravel may need topping up now and then to cover exposed patches of fabric. Secure the edges of the membrane with wire pins to prevent the frayed margins from surfacing. Gravel pathways must be able to cope with plenty of wear and tear, and it is advisable to lay the membrane first and then add the hardcore base and gravel topping to ensure that the fabric remains buried.

Stone chippings are made from crushed rock and come in a variety of colours. Large grades can look out of place in a domestic garden but smaller grades are effective. Slate chippings in plum, blue-grey or green work equally well in ultra-contemporary or semi-wild gardens, but this sharp-edged surfacing material is less forgiving than gravel when children fall on it. Chippings made from stone, glass, synthetic and recycled materials are laid in the same way as gravel.

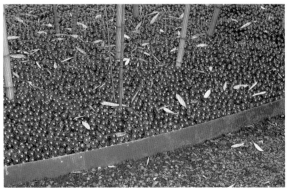

Opposite: *If you can, try to source and buy quantities of loose gravel or shingle direct from your local quarry site, cutting out the middleman. Ordering loose gravel from such a site will work out considerably cheaper than having to buy bagged material even from a builder's merchant.*

Top: *If you don't mind plants self-seeding occasionally, gravel paths and patios create a softness that perfectly complements flower beds.*

Above: *Novelty materials are now available, including the iridescent glass beads used here as mulch beside a striking blue glass flooring.*

lawns & ground cover

A well-kept lawn acts as a verdant foil for colourful flowerbeds and forms a visually restful open space, but other ground-cover choices are available if the growing conditions of your plot are not suited to grass.

Seed or turf classified as general-purpose is suitable for gardens used by children, and contains tough, coarse grasses such as perennial ryegrass that withstand wear and tear and recover quickly from moderate foot traffic and ball games. Weekly mowing and a couple of feed treatments during the growing season should keep it in reasonably good condition. The odd flowering weed is usually tolerated, and you can avoid watering if you delay mowing during dry periods and raise the cutting height to protect the grass roots from scorching.

Coarse grasses are not suitable if you want to create a show lawn or bowling green. This is the other extreme in terms of maintenance, and you will need a mixture that contains fine, slow-growing grasses such as fescues and bents. Lawns of this nature need to be mown twice a week with the blades on a low setting, and should be fed routinely and sometimes even irrigated during the hot summer months. Provided water restrictions are not in place, run sprinklers long enough for the water to penetrate deeply, as frequent light watering encourages surface rooting, which will make the turf more vulnerable to scorching in hot weather.

A striped effect on a lawn is achieved using a mower with a rear roller; generally, a cylinder mower is considered to give the best-quality cut, provided it is properly serviced. Other treatments for the lawn might include weed and moss control; rolling; scarifying to remove dead thatch; dispersing worm casts with a besom prior to mowing, and aerating to improve drainage.

Seed mixtures are now available for shady lawns but, in general, grass dislikes shade, particularly when it is created by overhanging trees or tall hedges because the ground tends to be dry and impoverished. In this case, try some other form of ground-cover planting that is better suited to the conditions. Suitable examples include evergreens such as the

plain green forms of English ivy (*Hedera helix*), *Pachysandra terminalis* and *Euphorbia amygdaloides* var. *robbiae*. Mosses and liverworts will colonize shady lawns and areas with poor drainage. Although moss killers are available, the moss will quickly return unless the underlying problem is dealt with effectively. In a moist, shaded area of the lawn, consider replacing turf with *Lamium maculatum* cultivars and *Epimedium* species, while in dry, sunny areas try low-growing aromatic herbs, such as creeping thymes, marjorams and lawn chamomile (*Chamaemelum nobile* 'Treneague'). Close-planted dwarf lavender and cotton lavender will also produce a better result than grass in such a sun-drenched location.

OPPOSITE: *The sharp contrast between mown lawn and long grass colonized by wildflowers, such as this ox-eye daisy, is visually pleasing. Setting aside less cultivated areas will also create a wildlife habitat.*

ABOVE: *Some ground-cover plants are more suitable than grass for places such as the dry shade beneath trees, poorly drained areas or garden hot spots, such as here, where stipa and sage make an attractive carpet.*

index

Picture Acknowledgements
The Publishers would
like to thank **Jenny
Hendy** for the use of
her photographs on
pages 3, 6, 10, 13, 19b,
25, 26b, 28t, 29bl, 36,
37t, 45, 46tl, 47, 48,
62 and 63.